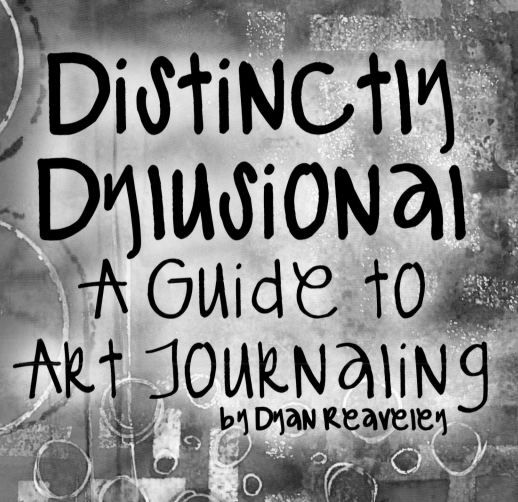

Distinctly Dylusional

A Guide to Art Journaling

by Dyan Reaveley

MW00609746

I hope you all enjoy this book.
My philosophy is...
Life is hard, your art shouldn't be!

Ryan
xx.

2

Table of Contents

What is Art Journaling

To me there is no set definition of art journaling. I didn't realise I was an art journaler until people started calling me one. I just have journals that I do my art in! I have many on the go at the same time, all shapes and sizes. No idea why I have so many, I just have this overriding desire to take blank journals and fill them with art. It doesn't matter where I am or what I am doing, I would rather be working in a journal. You have no idea how many times I wanted to stop writing this book to go and play in my journal!!! How I finished it, is amazing to everyone, I can tell you.

This obsession came about from my love of making backgrounds. For years, I have taught and demonstrated art techniques and I ended up with a growing mountain of decorated sheets of card. I started to fold these in half and glue them together into journals, adding tags etc. and just stroking them every now and then. Occasionally I would stamp in them or write a little quote, but apart from that I had no idea what else to do with them.

Then, early 2009 my Mum died very unexpectedly. We had no warning. It just happened and my world fell to pieces. I had lost my Dad seven years earlier and to lose both parents at an early age just seemed so unfair. I was angry and hurt and confused and didn't know where to turn. Because it was unexpected, I still had teaching commitments to fulfill. The first being 2 days after her death. I just had to put my "mask" on and get on with it.

I was flicking through a magazine and happened upon a picture of a woman with sunglasses on and it really resonated with me, so I cut it out and stuck it into one of my home-made journals. Then another picture, then another and another. And then I wrote around the pictures. I wrote everything that was in my heart; who I was, what I felt, how angry I was, how life was so unfair...and the floodgates opened and I couldn't stop. It was during this period that I eventually sought professional help for a lot of my issues and was finally diagnosed and treated, and it is all there in my early journals. The despair, the encouragement, the hope and the journey. Through therapy and my journals, I went deep down into myself and emerged out the other side with a deeper, more thorough understanding of who and what I was. I learnt that I needed to value myself. So I gave myself space in my journals away from self criticism, time to understand who I was and more importantly I gave myself a time and a place to heal. The therapeutic value of my journals is extremely difficult to put into words but, suffice to say, I believe they have shaped me into the woman I am today. I am passionate about introducing the therapeutic value of art journaling to everyone and I travel the world teaching and extolling its virtues. These days I cannot imagine being without a journal. In fact, the thought terrifies me. They have become so much a part of me and I carry them everywhere. It's very rare that a day goes by without me adding a little something to one of them. They are as important to my soul as oxygen is to my brain and I know without them I wouldn't know what to do.

Reasons To Art Journal

There are many reasons why someone would keep an art journal. As I explained, mine was started as a place to try out techniques all in one place, which quickly became a place to express my thoughts and feelings. Maybe you too want to journal for the therapeutic benefits, or maybe you are going traveling and want to keep a record of where you go and what you see.

The very first journals were in diary form and many people still do the same today. Many famous people's journals are now there for all of us to read and see the evolution of their lives, e.g. Anne Frank, Samuel Pepys. I never kept a diary for longer than a week but a look back through my journals I will tell you everything you need to know.

Keeping your art together in one place enables you to see the progression you have made. Many artists throughout the centuries kept notebooks where they did practise sketches and could see the improvements to their work and many artists today are carrying on this tradition, whether consciously or not.

You might not feel that you are an artist, but we are ALL artists, some better than others. If you can pick up a pencil and make a mark onto paper, then you are an artist. Do you remember the joy of watching a child filling a blank piece of paper with scribble "drawings"? Or dipping a brush into paint and making bold strokes across a blank canvas? Ask them if they are an artist and the answer is an overwhelming yes. My 8 year old granddaughter is a fabulous artist and one of the reasons is she believes herself to be and has never been told otherwise. She doesn't have one ounce of self doubt. She believes in herself and that's all that matters.

I believe in myself
and that's all that matters.

YOU need to believe in YOURSELF
because that's all that matters.

However and whatever
you create in your journal,
do it because you love it!

Tools of the Trade: Surfaces, Journals & Tags

My favourite place to work is in my Dylusions Creative Journal. The paper in there was created specifically to work with my line of products. The large and small journals contain a heavyweight, durable Mixed Media Cardstock that stands up to all of my Ink Spray and painting techniques. If I need to make something outside of my journals, I will use Ranger's Mixed Media Cardstock which is loose 8 ½" x 11" sheets of the same fabulous paper.

The journal pages are stitched in signatures and are really heavy duty. My journals take some battering but the kraft hard cover softens over time like an old leather sofa. The inside of each journal contains a large envelope where I keep all my tags, collage cut outs, quote books and my journal block, all at hand.

I love working on manila tags themselves, mainly the large no. 10's and 12's. Many of these end up on a journal page, but they are also invaluable for folding and making into a mini book. Lightly primed canvas is a fabulous surface to work on, but it dries quick so you need to work fast.

Tools of the Trade: Inks & Paints

My Dylusions Ink Sprays are made specifically to my requirements and I use them on 95% of my artwork. Mainly all over as a background, but also on top as surface decoration. They are reactive with water and therefore never permanent. They also contain a retardant which enables me to remove some of the dye from the page.

The main thing for me when using a paint in my journal is that it has to be water-based and dry to a matte finish. I have to be able to doodle and journal over the top with pens. My favourite are my Dylusions Paints: my vibrant colors in a wide-mouth jar perfect for dipping baby wipes and Craft Scrapers into. I also love to use Dina Wakley Media Paint: slightly creamy, buttery paints that dry to a smooth matte finish, ensuring your pages don't stick together. My other go to paints are Distress Paints. Very fluid, fast drying, and opaque with a myriad of colours to choose from.

Tools of the Trade: Stamps & Stencils

I am an old stamper as they say and I can't imagine not using them on my journal pages. I mainly use cling mounted rubber stamps as they are far more convenient. Stamps are fabulous for those who can't draw and also when you are in a hurry. Clear Stamps also are amazing as they are see-through, making it easier for positioning.

Where would I be without stencils? I use them on practically everything I do - for ghosting, adding top texture, doodling through, etc. In my line there are 2 sizes of each design, large and small. All are made from sturdy translucent plastic. My silhouette stencils and my Suits and Shapes stencils also include the cut out shapes which I use for masking techniques.

Tools of the Trade: Pens & Brushes

The majority of the pens I use are just black and white for all my doodling and writing. The most important thing to me is that they must be water-resistant when dry. This gives me endless possibilities for layering on my pages. I have a list of my favourites in the journaling section of this book. I also love coloured paint pens for adding pop to images.

The majority of my colouring in is done with the Tim Holtz Detailer Tip Waterbrushes filled with Dylusions Ink Sprays, straight from the bottle, with a Pipette. These go everywhere with me, even onto the aeroplane, where you will often find me colouring. I love the vibrancy and they match my backgrounds perfectly.

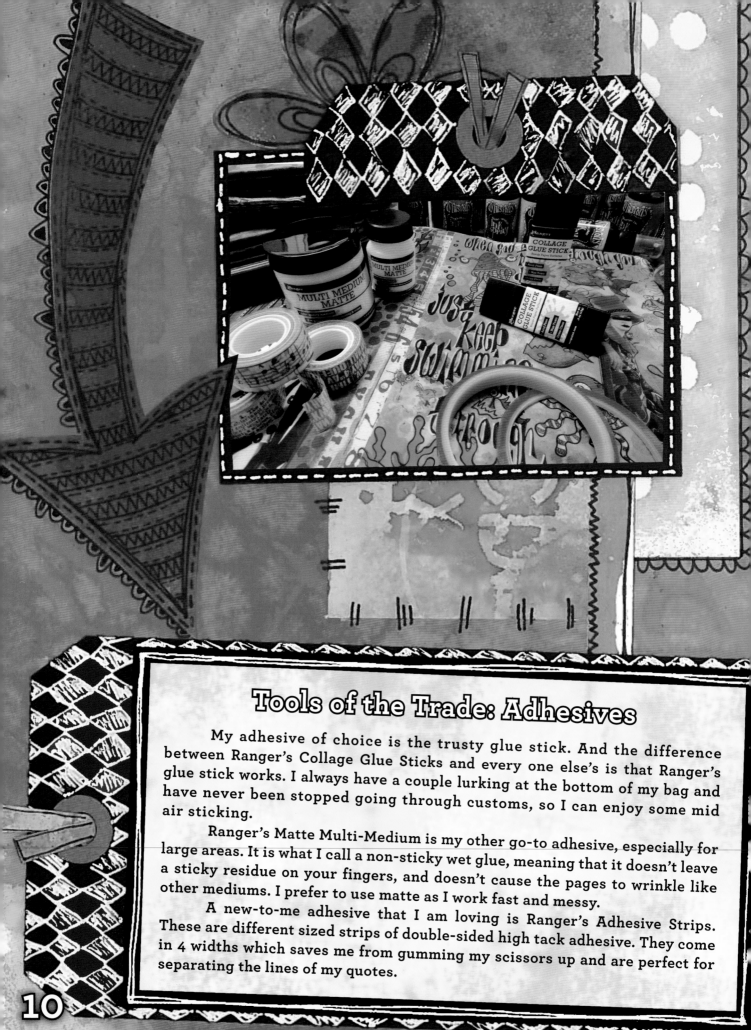

Tools of the Trade: Adhesives

My adhesive of choice is the trusty glue stick. And the difference between Ranger's Collage Glue Sticks and every one else's is that Ranger's glue stick works. I always have a couple lurking at the bottom of my bag and have never been stopped going through customs, so I can enjoy some mid air sticking.

Ranger's Matte Multi-Medium is my other go-to adhesive, especially for large areas. It is what I call a non-sticky wet glue, meaning that it doesn't leave a sticky residue on your fingers, and doesn't cause the pages to wrinkle like other mediums. I prefer to use matte as I work fast and messy.

A new-to-me adhesive that I am loving is Ranger's Adhesive Strips. These are different sized strips of double-sided high tack adhesive. They come in 4 widths which saves me from gumming my scissors up and are perfect for separating the lines of my quotes.

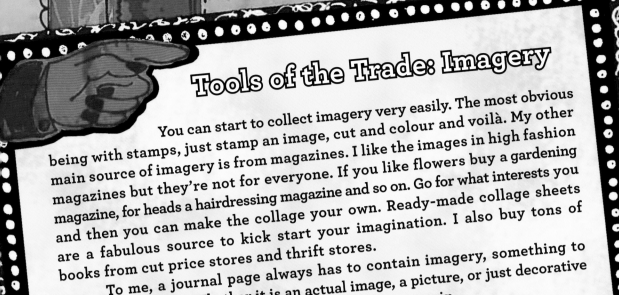

Tools of the Trade: Imagery

You can start to collect imagery very easily. The most obvious being with stamps, just stamp an image, cut and colour and voilà. My other main source of imagery is from magazines. I like the images in high fashion magazines but they're not for everyone. If you like flowers buy a gardening magazine, for heads a hairdressing magazine and so on. Go for what interests you and then you can make the collage your own. Ready-made collage sheets are a fabulous source to kick start your imagination. I also buy tons of books from cut price stores and thrift stores.

To me, a journal page always has to contain imagery, something to focus your eye on. Whether it is an actual image, a picture, or just decorative wording. The page needs something to draw your eye in.

Tools of the Trade: Basics

Dylusions Ink Spray Pad
A blank, hinged-top pad for the purpose of filling with ink sprays to create your own custom colour ink pad. Ink to use. Can be rinsed out to use with other colours.

Scissors
My scissor of choice is the Tim Holtz Tonic Scissors. The smaller pair for all my fiddly fancy cutting and the larger pair for straight edges and fabric.

Dylusions Journal Block
The Dylusions Journal Block is a multi-functional acrylic block. Its' main purpose is to mount the Dylusions Stamps onto. The wavy edge makes it easy to hold and also doubles as a creative edge for drawing around. I added the inch measurements to the straight-edge as I can never find my ruler.

Ranger Nonstick Craft Sheet
Not sure how I would manage all my inky goodness without a Craft Sheet. In my opinion it is the only surface to work on and everything in my studio is covered in it.

Ranger Mister
Most of my techniques require water and I like to use the same bottle and sprayer that my inks are in. It gives me just the right spray I need, not too little and not too much.

Tapes
As I tear pages out of my book to move them around, I need to tape them back in. My favourite tape is tissue tape as it is easy to tear and quite translucent, enabling the underneath to show through. I also like some washi tapes but find it a bit of a minefield choosing as there are so many on the market. My tape of choice at the moment is masking tape, always loved the plain to stamp on, but especially loving the bright new colours that are everywhere to be seen. I use it to attach tags and envelopes. Rather than keep it smooth, I tend to add it scrumpled.

Ranger Craft Scraper
This small tool does a multitude of jobs and is always near me. I use it to spread paint, create graphic lines, to flick paint, as a bone folder and also to clean a messy Craft Sheet.

Brayer
Invaluable for rolling over stencils to get the best results.

Baby Wipes
Again, to me, these are an important part of my work so I like to buy water-based hypoallergenic wipes. Again, they need to be sturdy enough to withstand my not so gentle treatment.

Kitchen Roll
Used to remove excess ink from journal pages. Buy the best you can afford. It is as much a tool as anything else and poor quality will give poor results!

Anatomy of a Page

So where do we start? There are five (love me an odd number) key elements that I use when creating journal pages:

Backgrounds
Borders
Imagery
Doodling
Journaling

The purpose of this book is to break each of these elements down into easy to follow steps, giving you a tried and tested formula to use. A bit like having basic ingredients in your kitchen cupboard. Using some or all of these basic ingredients and adding in pinches of this and spoonfuls of that will guarantee a different result every time. There are so many ways to create each of these individual elements and over the next few pages, I will be showing you many of the different techniques I use and explaining each of the processes. I very, very rarely make a journal page from start to finish. I tend to be quite repetitive in what I do, building up the layers of many pages at once. My studio is where I tend to do all my inking and the basics of my backgrounds. It is also where I do most of my stamping and borders.

Assembling imagery can be done anywhere as I always carry around a file full of stamped and cut out images, and a couple of glue sticks. Doodling and journaling are normally reserved for those periods where I can spend a long time without interruption, for example on my many frequents jaunts in an aeroplane. I have passed many a long journey, from airport to airport, engrossed in my journals. The biggest questions I get asked are: Where do you start? What order do you do things? Do you do one page at a time or have a few on the go? Answers - You start at the beginning and after awhile you find your own way of working. Over time, I realized that I have a certain order to the way I compile my pages, one that I nearly always stick to. So I decided to break it down for you to follow. I call this "Anatomy of a Page".

Background Basics:
What is a background?

In all of my journal pages the background is as equally important to me as any of the focal points that I may put on top even though you don't see as much of it. To me it is the scalfolding that you build your structure around, but it should not detract from your focal point. Often when I am looking at new journalers' work, it can be hard to see where the focal point of the page is. This is because there is too much going on in the background. A background is called a background because it is IN the background!!! Always try to remember this. It should not be trying to compete with your main image, the focal point of your page. If your background is too busy it is difficult to distinguish between it and what you want to stand out. Ideally your eye should go straight to the focal point of your page and then take in the background detail.

My method of getting my backgrounds to have a really cohesive look is to use three inks from either the cool family or the warm family. When adding more layers to the basic background, I still concentrate on only those three colours. This ensures that your background doesn't become too overpowering and that everything is on their equal space.

I never add other colours apart from black or white elements because black and white are not officially "colours". They will always make your colours pop. I very rarely make one background at a time. I actually prefer to make a whole bunch in one session. My theory is if you're going to get messy you might as well get good and messy! I usually fill at least a quarter of a journal, plus loose pages, in one session. I start by inking them all and putting them to one side, then going back and ghosting them. By the time I have finished the last page most of the other pages are already dry and ready to add more layers of ink. I can ink, ghost and add layers for a couple of hours, which ensures that I always have a good supply of backgrounds available to start working on.

Background Basics:
Colour Theory: Cool & Warm

Ink Sprays work differently than other mediums. Because they can cover a large area and two colours can easily become combined, it is important to understand which colours work together. It is all too easy to take beautifully bright colours and make mud.

Many colours opposite to each other on a colour wheel can easily make mud, e.g. orange and blue, yellow and purple, red and green. The simplest way to avoid this is to divide the inks into two collections, cool colours and warm colours.

Any of the colours included in the warm collection will blend together beautifully, as will any of the colours included in the cool collection. Therefore the basis of my backgrounds are created in either cool or warm. It is extremely rare that I mix inks from both collections.

Cool Collection
The cool colours are those which remind me of being out at sea, the greeny blues. There are 10 colours in this collection: Lemon Zest, Fresh Lime, Cut Grass, Dirty Martini, Polished Jade, Crushed Pesto, London Blue, Vibrant Turquoise, Calypso Teal and After Midnight.

Warm Collection
The warm colours remind me of being all cozy in front of a raging fire, the oranges and reds. There are 10 colours in this collection: Pure Sunshine, Squeezed Orange, Tangerine Dream, Postbox Red, Cherry Pie, Pomegranate Seed, Bubblegum Pink, Funky Fuchsia, Melted Chocolate and Ground Coffee.

Crushed Grape
There is one colour which flips between the two categories and that is Crushed Grape. In the cool collection it looks fabulous with any of the blues, but dreadful with greens or yellow. In the warm collection it looks fabulous with reds and pinks but dreadful with yellow and orange. Once you understand how your inks work you will get crisp bright colours every time.

Neutrals/Staples
There are 3 other Ink Sprays in my line that I call staples which go with anything. These are Black Marble, White Linen and Slate Grey.

Ghosting

My Ink Sprays are especially made for the way I work. They are water-based and translucent, which means I can layer them over each other and they are packed with tons of intense dyes giving them real vibrancy. I like a really blended look and to achieve this, I spray large puddles of ink onto the surface I am working on. I only ever use three colours at a time as I feel too many can look a bit busy. Adding a light spritz of water to the paper first ensures that the colours absorb evenly without giving a patchy finish. Because I use a lot of ink to achieve this look and don't want to waste any, I always take another page or tag and place on top of the inked surface pressing down lightly to transfer the ink. This gives you two surfaces to play with.

Ghosting is a name I came up with for the technique I use for removing ink with my stencils and water, because it gives an imperfect ghost-like image. My inks are not permanent and are reactive with water, meaning I can remove some of the dye from the background. This can be done at any time, as soon as the page is inked, a week later, a month later, a year later! Although the ink is dry it will never be permanent, so be warned if you spill your coffee on an inked page you will have an interesting result. Some of my best pages have tea drips or Margarita spills on them, lol.

I like to spritz water through a stencil to create a positive image and then flip the wet stencil over, pressing down to make a negative image. I love the juxtaposition these two opposites make. After lifting the stencils I would roll over firmly with the kitchen roll to remove the ink. The stencil will have picked up a bit of the reactivated ink and so I always clean it by pressing it down onto a page in my journal.

Supplies Used:

Dylusions Creative Journal
Dylusions Ink Sprays
Ranger Mister
Dylusions Stencil
Kitchen Roll

Ghosting

1. Spritz the page with water.

2. Spray a large puddle of ink in two areas of the page.

5. Peel the pages apart and blot with the kitchen roll.

6. Lay a stencil over half of the page and spritz through with water.

3. Repeat this with two more colours of ink and lightly spritz with water to blend.

4. Place another journal page on the top and press down firmly to transfer the excess ink.

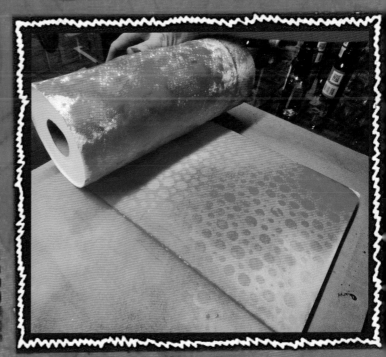

7. Lift the stencil and flip it over onto the other half of the page. Press down firmly and remove.

8. Blot the page to reveal the ghosted image.

Building Layers

When adding ink layers to a ghosted background I only use the colours I originally used to create it, going from light to dark, layering them on top of each other. Because my inks are translucent you can easily see the layers. I personally never use a contrast colour as I find it too distracting in a background.

I work from light to dark, as it is easier to add more colour than remove it. I take the background part of a large stencil and place it on an inked and dried page and with the lightest of the inks used, I lightly spritz through a portion of the stencil. Be careful of spritzing through too much ink as it will seep under the design. I pick up the inky stencil and flip it over, pressing down lightly to transfer. I then reflip, place on a different part of the page and lightly spritz through again. Blot the ink with the kitchen roll. I call this the spritz, flip, spritz, blot.

Using a different large background stencil and the medium colour of ink I repeat this process across the page. For the darkest colour of ink I switch to a smaller sized background stencil. This time I will use a smaller portion of the stencil but in more areas of the page. If your page is quite dark you could use Slate Grey or Black Marble as your darkest colour. If your page is really dark you could use White Linen ink, to lift and lighten. Because black and white aren't really considered colours, you can add these on top of any of your inked pages. At first they look as though they are going to stand out but most stamping and writing is done in black so it becomes a neutral and everything blends.

Supplies Used:

The Same 3 Dylusions Ink Sprays used in the Background

Large & Small Dylusions Background Stencils

Kitchen Roll

Building Layers

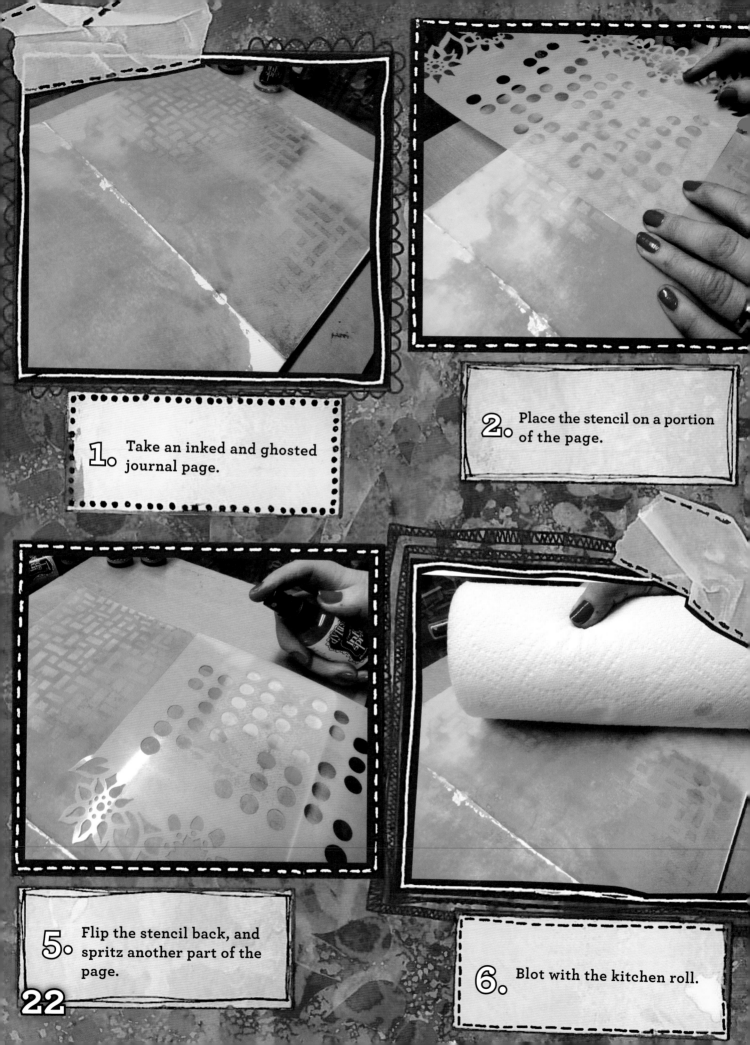

1. Take an inked and ghosted journal page.

2. Place the stencil on a portion of the page.

5. Flip the stencil back, and spritz another part of the page.

6. Blot with the kitchen roll.

3. Of the three colours used originally, pick the lightest colour and spritz through a portion of the stencil.

4. Flip the stencil over and press down to transfer the ink onto the page.

7. Repeat with another ink and a different stencil.

8. Repeat with a smaller stencil and the darkest ink.

23

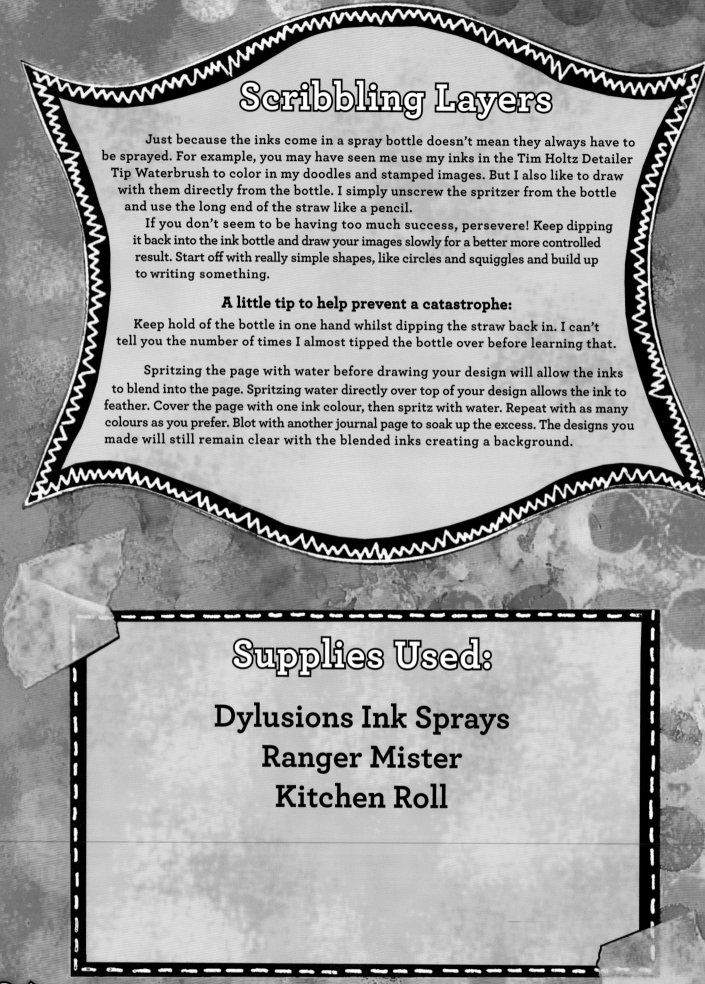

Scribbling Layers

Just because the inks come in a spray bottle doesn't mean they always have to be sprayed. For example, you may have seen me use my inks in the Tim Holtz Detailer Tip Waterbrush to color in my doodles and stamped images. But I also like to draw with them directly from the bottle. I simply unscrew the spritzer from the bottle and use the long end of the straw like a pencil.

If you don't seem to be having too much success, persevere! Keep dipping it back into the ink bottle and draw your images slowly for a better more controlled result. Start off with really simple shapes, like circles and squiggles and build up to writing something.

A little tip to help prevent a catastrophe:

Keep hold of the bottle in one hand whilst dipping the straw back in. I can't tell you the number of times I almost tipped the bottle over before learning that.

Spritzing the page with water before drawing your design will allow the inks to blend into the page. Spritzing water directly over top of your design allows the ink to feather. Cover the page with one ink colour, then spritz with water. Repeat with as many colours as you prefer. Blot with another journal page to soak up the excess. The designs you made will still remain clear with the blended inks creating a background.

Supplies Used:

Dylusions Ink Sprays
Ranger Mister
Kitchen Roll

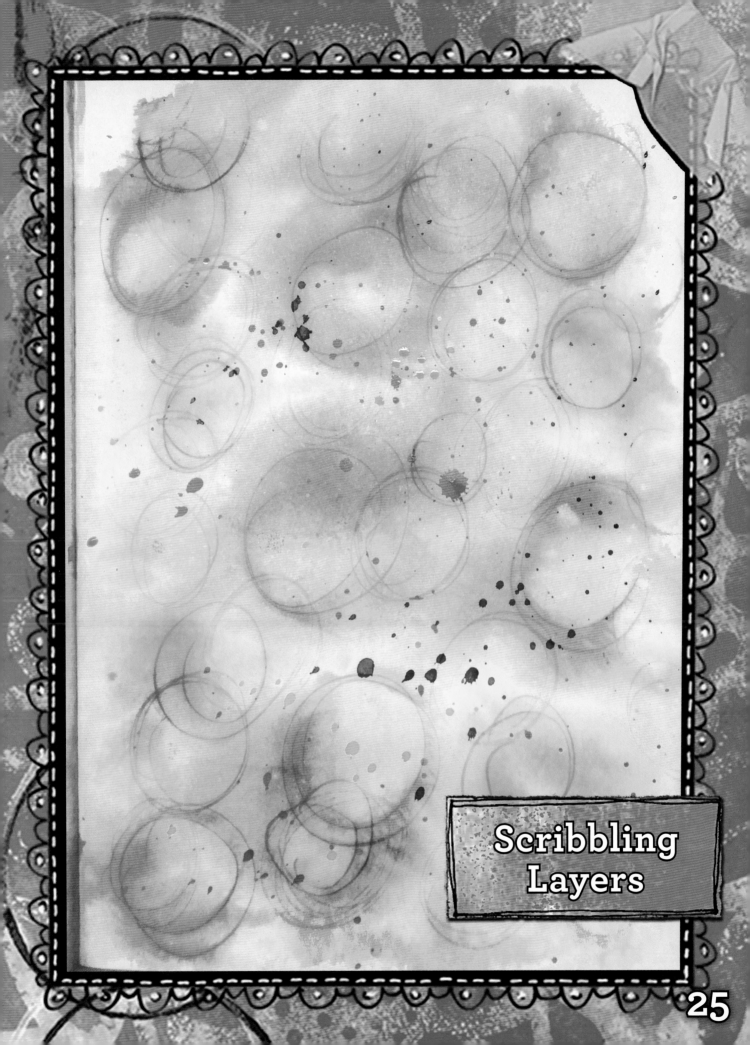

Scribbling
Layers

1. Spritz half a page with water. Remove the lid of an ink spray and draw circles.

2. Spritz over the ink with water to cause the ink to feather out.

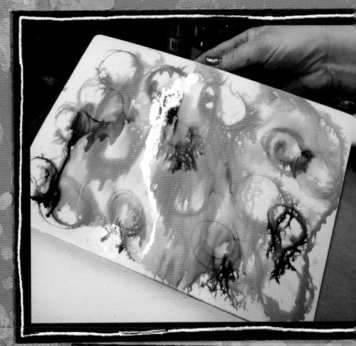

5. Repeat with as many colours as you like.

6. Pick up the page to let the colours run and bleed with each other.

3. Repeat this on the other half of the page.

4. Add a second colour of ink and spritz.

7. Blot with another journal page and kitchen roll and let dry.

8. Add extra texture by flicking ink onto the page and let dry.

Pastels

I adore bright colours but too much of the same can start to look a bit samey samey. I experiment a lot at home mixing different inks together in their bottles and also directly onto the page. Adding black creates earthtones and adding white creates vibrant pastels. Now I know that sounds a bit of a paradox, a vibrant pastel, but trust me! The White Linen Ink Spray is the only one in the collection that isn't translucent. It is a semi-opaque ink. This means it has pigment particles in it.

Now, the best way to describe this bottle of ink is to liken it to a snow globe, with the pigment particles being the snow. Every time you shake a snow globe the snow swirls round and blends with the liquid. In a snow globe the liquid remains clear but with my ink the liquid absorbs into the pigment making it milky white. When you place a snow globe down to rest the snow resettles on the bottom of the globe, similarly when you lay down the bottle of ink the pigment particles start to settle on the bottom of the bottle. This means that to get the true effect you need to shake the bottle every time you go to use it. Because the ink is a semi-opaque it picks up the colour of the other inks. For example, if you spray it onto a red inked background it will start to turn pink.

So, for fabulously vibrant pastels, I first spray a good coating of White Linen all over a journal page, making sure it is fully covered. I then lightly spritz a few colours of ink onto this. The colour bleeds out across the page. When I am happy with the amount of colour, I then tip the page up and let the inks start to run. You can always spritz on a little water to assist with this. The final step is to place another journal page over the top to mop up the excess ink, peel apart and blot. The result is pastel shades with a wonderful vibrancy about them. These pages can be ghosted to lift some of the ink out and layers can be added on the top also.

Supplies Used:

Dylusions White Linen Ink Spray
Dylusions Colours of Ink Sprays
Ranger Mister
Dylusions Stencils
Kitchen Roll

Pastels

29

1. Firmly shake the bottle of White Linen ink to mix.

2. Cover the page completely with a good layer of white.

5. Spritz lightly with water so colours start to blend.

6. Lift up the page to encourage the ink to run, and spritz again with water.

3. Lightly add small spritzes of a colour of ink.

4. Continue adding colours of ink until you are happy.

7. Place another journal page on the top to transfer the excess ink.

8. Blot excess ink off the page with kitchen roll.

Painting

Paint is another medium that I love to use. It is a quick and easy way to add colour all over a journal page. Although there are many types of paint on the market I always, always choose an acrylic paint. These are water-based paints, which have a good ol' amount of pigment in them. As with a lot of other things, you get what you pay for. If you buy a really cheap paint, it contains little pigment and therefore you have to use three times as much if not more. A good quality paint should allow you to keep the richness whilst only using a small amount. I like to use a matte finish paint, as I personally prefer the finished look in my journal. A gloss finish can be difficult to write over.

I very rarely use a brush to add my paint, as I find it takes too long to dry, preferring to use my Ranger Craft Scraper, baby wipes, Ranger Ink Blending Tool or even just my fingers. All of these ways are quick-drying enabling me to start with my collaging, etc. Applying with a Craft Scraper gives bold swathes of colour across your pages, but also enables the colours to layer over each other. Pick up some paint and hold the scraper as low to the page as you can and push down towards you. Repeating as necessary. Using a baby wipe gives a soft blended look to the paint. The baby wipe keeps the paint moist and easy to move around. Don't skrimp on your baby wipes, buy the best you can afford, it will be worth the extra pennies. To add more depth to the page, I add paint with a baby wipe and then blend with my fingers.

When going for a blended look I always use shades of the same colour, a light, a medium and a dark. I apply the light colour all over the page, then blend some of the medium colour in places and the darkest around the edge for framing. When applying with a craft scraper the paint dries very quickly so I can use contrasting colours, without fear of making mud. Because acrylic paint is a water-based medium, you can layer anything over the top of them: inks, pencils, markers, mediums, etc. And everything is easy to clean as well! Bonus.

Supplies Used:

Dylusions Paint
Ranger Craft Scraper
Dylusions Stencils
Baby Wipes
Kitchen Roll

Painting

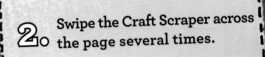

Painting with a Craft Scraper

1. Dip the Craft Scraper directly into the Dylusions Paint jar to apply paint.

2. Swipe the Craft Scraper across the page several times.

Blending with a Baby Wipe

1. Apply your lightest colour of paint onto page and blend with a baby wipe.

2. Choose a medium colour of paint and blend with baby wipe and hands.

3. Repeat with other colours and let dry.

4. Place stencil over and spray ink through, then blot.

3. Apply the deepest colour of paint with a blending tool around the edges for a frame.

4. Place stencil over page and spray ink through, then blot.

Stained Glass

One of my favourite things to do as a child was to draw shapes onto a piece of paper and then colour them all in different colours. This is my grown up version and one of the reasons I designed the shattered stencil. The negative image is needed for the design, so first of all you need to lay the stencil onto a new journal page and evenly spray over the design with Black Marble Ink Spray. Carefully lift up the stencil and flip it onto a new journal page. Make sure you haven't used too much ink as it will start to drip. Carefully press down over the top with the kitchen roll to transfer the ink. Lift the stencil and blot. This is the page we will be working on. I always give the stencil a light spritz with water and transfer any remaining ink onto another journal page for later. If you are going to clean, you might as well clean in your journal! I always put the page aside to dry thoroughly before doing any more. When it is dry, I take one or two of the silhouette stencils and paint around them with a black dabber. I soften the edges with a baby wipe leaving a lot of the background showing. Remove the masks and if you lightly spritz them with water you can clean the images right in your journal by laying them painty side down and pressing firmly.

I like to use a black pen to neaten up all the edges, my favourite is the Sakura Glaze as it leaves a slightly raised embossed look. Now is the fun part, the colouring in of the shapes. I colour everything in with my Ink Sprays filled with a Pipette into the Tim Holtz Detailer Tip Waterbrush. I choose one colour and fill in shapes of both figures and the remaining exposed area. When I'm happy, I choose another colour and do the same. Repeat this until you have coloured in every area. To make everything pop I then outline all the black lines with a white pen. The stained glass effect is one of my favourite things to finish whilst flying. I get so engrossed and before I know it I am at my destination.

Supplies Used:
Dylusions Shattered Large Stencil
Dylusions Black Marble Paint
Dylusions Ink Sprays
Tim Holtz Detailer Tip Waterbrush
Black & White Pens
Ranger Mister
Kitchen Roll

Stained Glass

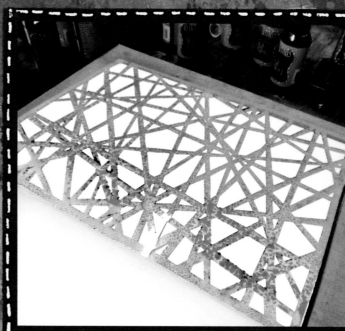

1. Take the large shattered stencil and place on a journal page. Spray all over evenly with black ink.

2. Lift the stencil and carefully flip over onto another journal page. Press down to transfer the ink. Blot and let dry.

5. Leave to dry then outline the edges with a black pen to neaten.

6. Take an ink filled detailer water-brush and colour in various shapes within the silhouette and border.

3. Place a large Dylusions silhouette mask and paint around it with Black Marble Dylusions Paint.

4. Place another mask at the side and repeat. Soften the edges with a baby wipe.

7. Repeat with more colours until all the shapes are filled.

8. Outline around the black with a white pen.

Dylusions
Ink Spray Pad Printing

For a long time I have wanted an inked pad that when stamped would give a variegated ink look. Not like the stripy rainbow pads you see. I wanted it to be more random. This was proving difficult as in a normal ink pad the colours would bleed together. I came up with the idea of a blank pad that you can mix your own colours on to. I usually use no more than three colours at a time, just like when I ink a page or tag. These can be any combination of colours you like but you get the best results if you stay within the warm or cool collections.

Because you are not overloading the pad with ink, the colours stay where you place them, so that when you stamp you see all the colours individually. The beauty of the pad is you can wash it out and reuse it with other colours. My Ink Sprays are not permanent and can be removed with water. Just take it and run it under the tap until the water turns clear. The pad may have some staining from the dye but it is ready for you to re-ink with more colours.

The pad can be used with stamps, my favourite are background script and graphic images, but it can also be used directly into your journal for a direct to paper look or for pressing through a stencil. Because we are working onto a dry page, part of the ink soaks into the paper straight away leaving the stamped image. If we spray water or polish with a baby wipe, we reactivate only the ink that is on the surface so we can still see the image underneath.

Supplies Used:

Dylusions Ink Spray Pad
Dylusions Ink Sprays
Dylusions Stencil
Ranger Mister
Brayer
Baby Wipes

Dylusions
Ink Spray Pad
Printing

41

Filling & Stamping

1. Lightly mist the pad with water and knead lightly to break the seal.

2. Spray three colours of ink onto the pad exactly as if you were inking a page.

Ink Spray Pad Printing

1. Spritz the stamped page with water.

2. Allow the ink to bleed and then blot with the kitchen roll.

3. Press stamp onto one part of the pad and stamp onto the journal page. Repeat, always using the same part of the pad to ink.

4. Stamp onto a different part of the pad and fill in the gaps to give a variegated inked look.

3. Take a baby wipe and gently polish the page.

4. This will give you an inked background but the stamped image will still be clear.

Stencil Printing

1. Lay a stencil onto a journal page.

2. Take the Ink Spray Pad and press through the stencil.

Monoprint from a Stencil

1. Spritz the stencil from the last technique with water.

2. Place it onto a journal page, inky side down.

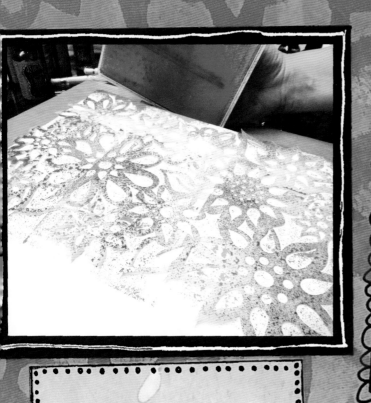

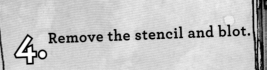

3. Repeat until the stencil is covered.

4. Remove the stencil and blot.

3. Roll over firmly with a brayer to transfer the ink.

4. Remove the stencil and blot.

Imagery Basics:
Why use Imagery?
What to look for?

I use a lot of imagery on my journal pages, the most obvious being stamps and magazine images; the less obvious being writing and doodling. Other types of imagery can be photos, postcards, maps; in fact any ephemera. It all depends what tools you use when creating a mental picture inside your head. There are many ways of doing this and we all do it differently. Each relates to a sense, feeling or action in the body...sight, hearing, touch, smell or feeling. If I asked you to think of an elephant and then describe it in as few words as possible, I usually have a good idea of which sense you use to feel things.

For example if you hear the elephants roar, your main tool is sound/hearing. If you mention the elephant's colour, your main tool is visual/seeing. Answers I have heard include, Africa, huge, grey, wrinkled, noisy, Dumbo, smelly. The type of imagery I use is visual and helps me tell the story of the page. Many of my pages have collage images as their focal point and I am asked all the time where I find such weird magazines to get them from. I have to laugh when I tell them they are not weird magazines, they are normal ones that you can buy in any store. I take the normal images from the normal magazines and use them in a weird way. Well, weird to some, obviously not to me, lol. I always separate the heads and legs from the bodies and reattach them onto other images. I use flowers and food for hair, I always change the eyes by adding glasses or a word on the top of them.

Over the next few pages I will be breaking imagery down and explaining the types I use so you can see how I would normally approach a journal page. Think of it as a menu where you can select all or some of the items to create your finished piece.

It's very rare that I have a journal page
without any images on it. On these
pages the imagery comes in the form
of decorative writing
and of course...
the ubiquitous doodling!

Imagery Basics:
Types

Magazine Images
I buy a variety of magazines from high-end women's fashion
to hair and tattoo and art and culture.
I flick through and if I find at least 10 images then it's mine, lol.
Find what interests you - garden magazines, hair, etc. and get cutting.

Collage Sheets
These are ready made sheets of images available hard copy or via download.
Most of the work has been done for you, ie. altering and doodling, but are fabulous
for kick starting your inspiration.

Books
Search through old book stores for interesting images, ie. butterflies to use as wings.
Try to think out of the box.

Scrapbook/Wrapping Paper
Both scrapbook paper and wrapping paper are a fabulous source for images to use
and regularly appear altered in my journal.

Stamps
Stamps are invaluable for providing imagery to your pages.
They can be used on their own or in conjunction with collage.

Stencils
Most stencils are mainly for background use, but I love to use ones with
the bigger images. Stenciling out your page with black and leaving the
image coming through looks stunning.

Old Photos
It can be really fun using old photos on your pages, I like to draw
bright new clothes on them and decorate with spots, stripes, etc.
When I don't have any photos on hand I use Tim Holtz Ideaology
Found Relatives Cards and fancy them up!

Borders

I like to use borders on many of my journal pages. I feel that it gives a finished and "framed" look to the piece. Personally, I wouldn't hang a picture on my wall without framing it first! I feel the same way about my journal pages.

There are many different ways I like to use to create borders, for example with stamps, doodles, and collage. If I am doodling a border, it is normally one of the last things I do. However, a stamped border is better applied first before any images. I will quite often spend some time adding stamped borders to pages so that they are ready for when I want to use them in the future. Many of my stamps are border images specifically made for this purpose. Some of them are made especially for you to be able to join up and make the border continuous around the page.

I always use a waterproof ink to stamp with so that I have the option of colouring in the images later. Another way of creating borders or frames is with the wavy edge of my Journal Block. I use this to draw decorative lines around the edges of pages just like many of the text blocks in this book. You will also often see a collaged border on my pages. I look for interesting textures on magazine pages and cut them into squares and oblongs and edge my page with them. Another tip is to try sticking to one colour family or just black and white. This really frames the page and directs your eye to the focal point.

Supplies Used:
Dylusions Border Stamps

Dylusions Journal Block

Ranger Jet Black Archival Ink

Tim Holtz Detailer Tip Waterbrushes filled with Dylusions Ink Sprays

Scrap Paper

Black Pen

Borders

1. Ink the border stamp with black ink and stamp along the top of the page.

2. Repeat at the bottom of the page.

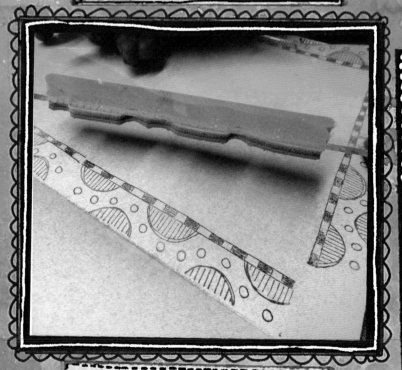

5. Repeat this step on the opposite side of the page.

6. With a black pen, draw in the checked lines.

3. Stamp down the side of the page, leaving a border size gap at the top.

4. Mask off the stamped border at the bottom with paper. Stamp over the paper joining borders.

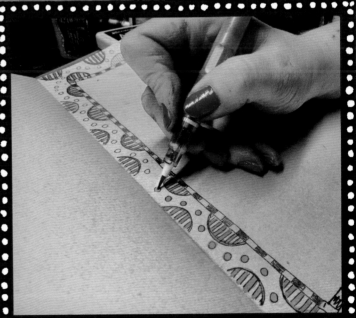

7. Draw in the remaining designs.

8. Colour in the shapes with the ink filled waterbrushes.

Stamps & Stencils

Stamps and stencils are invaluable tools for adding imagery to your pages. Stamping has seen a massive revival over the past decade and with the advent of cling-mounted and clear sets it has become a lot more affordable. Both of these types of stamps are mounted onto vinyl sheets and are easy to store. Both easily self-adhere to see-through acrylic blocks so you can easily position them on your page. I stamp background images directly onto the page, but for the main images I normally stamp them onto white or ivory cardstock and colour them in before cutting them out and sticking them on. I always have a file of stamped images ready to colour and use. If I am stamping one image that I need it is really quick to stamp another two and pop them into my file for later. To clean my stamp, I normally stamp over part of a journal page until there is no ink left. This then becomes part of the background for a new page.

Stencils have seen a massive resurgence in the last five years and are an invaluable tool for me in my journal; from adding ink to backgrounds, using as a doodling tool and creating main focal images. They are very light and easy to store and transport around. I always have an assortment tucked into the back of my journal for doodling on the go. You can use them with ink, paint, sprays, or pens to name a few. There are a range of silhouette stencils in my Dylusions line that also include the positive and negative images to be used as masks. These are fabulous for creating stunning focal points on a page.

Supplies Used:

Dylusions Silhouette Stencils & Masks
Black Marble Dylusions Paint
Text Stamp
Dylusions Journal Block
Ranger Jet Black Archival Ink
Black & White Pen

Stamps & Stencils

1. Stamp images onto white cardstock with Archival Ink.

2. Using a filled waterbrush colour in stamped images.

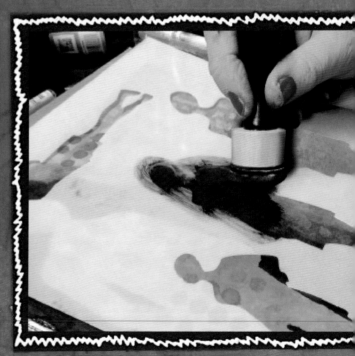

1. Place a silhouette mask onto one side of a journal page and paint over with Black Marble Dylusions Paint. Soften the edges with a baby wipe.

2. Place another silhouette stencil next to the image and paint through the stencil with a Mini Ink Blending tool.

3. Cut out the images.

4. Add to journal pages.

3. Place the correct stencil over the first image. Ink a stamp with black ink and stamp through the stencil. Repeat.

4. When dry, outline first with a black pen then with a white pen.

Faux Bleach Out

In my older days of stamping, we used bleach to take out some of the colour from a page. This was really effective but a little bit precarious. If you spilt the bleach on your clothes, they were ruined. As you can imagine, I ruined a fair few outfits! I also can't cope very well with the smell so my bleaching days were cut short. Because my inks are reactive with water, I wanted to see if I could get a similar effect to the bleach just using water alone. It worked fabulously and so I call it my faux bleach out. It works with any of the colours of my inks but the darker colours give a more dramatic result, which I love. I usually add a bright colour to a portion of the page and then black to the remainder and let it dry. I then stamp a design onto the black using a black waterproof ink pad. In this case, an open leaf design. For optimum results, you need to use a stamp that has a fair bit of area to colour in. With a detailer waterbrush filled with water, I paint in 3 to 4 leaves, leaving the water to sit for a few seconds before pressing down and blotting with a piece of kitchen roll. I then repaint those leaves and repaint a few more before pressing and blotting them all. The blotting will remove the ink from inside the leaf shape. I carry on painting, pressing and blotting, until each leaf has been painted twice. Any more than twice will damage the paper. Every now and then you need to wipe off the black ink that will have collected on the tip of the waterbrush. You can leave these images as they are, but I like to take a water brush with the same colour ink as the background and repaint the leaves. It looks as though the bright ink is appearing through the black. When all of the ink is thoroughly dry, I usually outline with a white pen to make the leaves really pop.

Supplies Used:

Dylusions Ink Sprays

Open Leaf Stamp

Tim Holtz Detailer Tip Waterbrushes filled with Dylusions Ink Sprays

White Pen

Kitchen Roll

Faux
Bleach Out

1. Spray a colour of ink onto a quarter of the page.

2. Spray the rest of the page with black ink, making sure both colours blend together. Blot with another page and let dry.

5. Paint the same four or five leaves again, plus four or five more and blot, to lift out the colour.

6. Work your way throughout the leaves, until you have "bleached" the colour from them all.

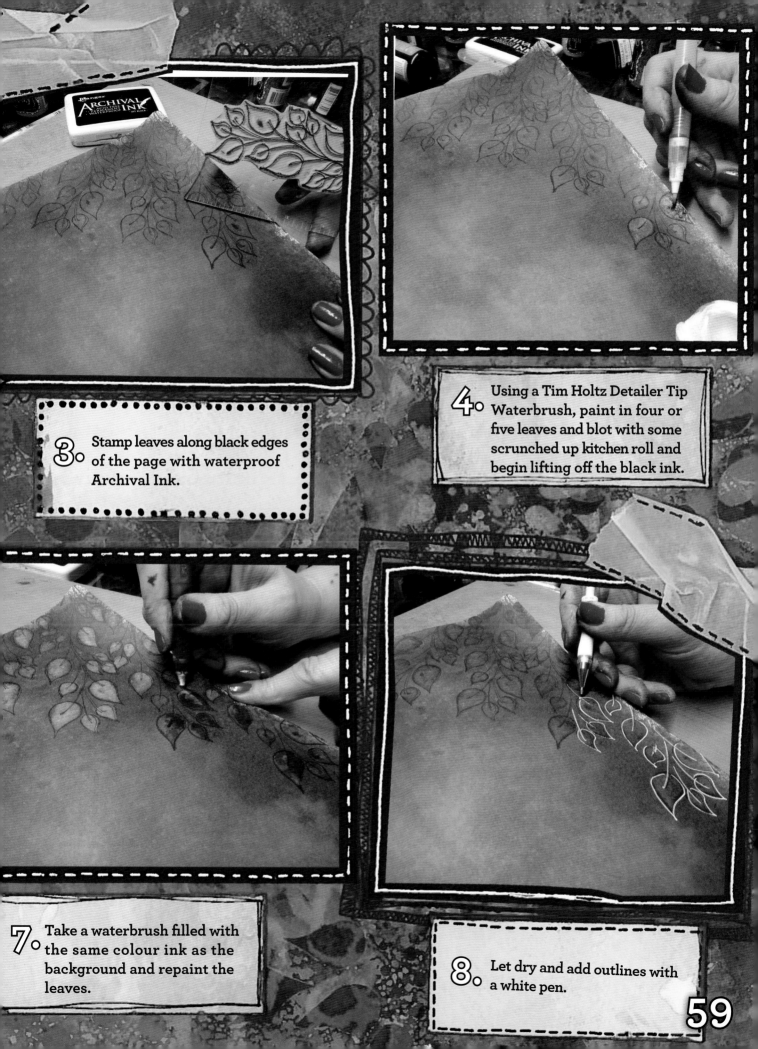

3. Stamp leaves along black edges of the page with waterproof Archival Ink.

4. Using a Tim Holtz Detailer Tip Waterbrush, paint in four or five leaves and blot with some scrunched up kitchen roll and begin lifting off the black ink.

7. Take a waterbrush filled with the same colour ink as the background and repaint the leaves.

8. Let dry and add outlines with a white pen.

Text Background

Text is a great way to add interest to a background, whether you write it yourself or use stamps or stencils. Contrary to popular belief, background writing is not meant to be read just to enhance. Most of what you write will be covered up by imagery. Once you realise this, you give yourself the freedom to write whatever you like. The fear of other people seeing what you write can be off putting, but it is really rare that anyone actually tries to read it. It just becomes a part of a decorative background.

Stamping in a complementary colour to the background will make it blend in more. A contrast colour or black will make it more prominent. There are tons of writing stamps on the market. My Dylusions word stamps are copies of my handwriting; these are useful to give you the look of having written it yourself. It is also a lot quicker to stamp than to write. You can add extra oomph by using a letter stencil. I frequently will add some black paint through one to lift a page.

Saying that, I do love the look of a background with writing all over. It is a simple and effective way of creating a striking look that no one can actually read. Again, this is good if you are not too sure about your handwriting as it will be really difficult to see clearly. The writing is just another form of decoration. Fill the page with writing from top to bottom, then turn the page 90 degrees and continue writing over the existing writing. I always use a water resistant pen just in case I want to add anything over the writing.

Supplies Used:

Text Stamps
Ranger Jet Black Archival Ink
Dylusions Alphabet Stencils
Black Marble Dylusions Paint
Water Resistant Black Pen
Ranger Mini Ink Blending Tool

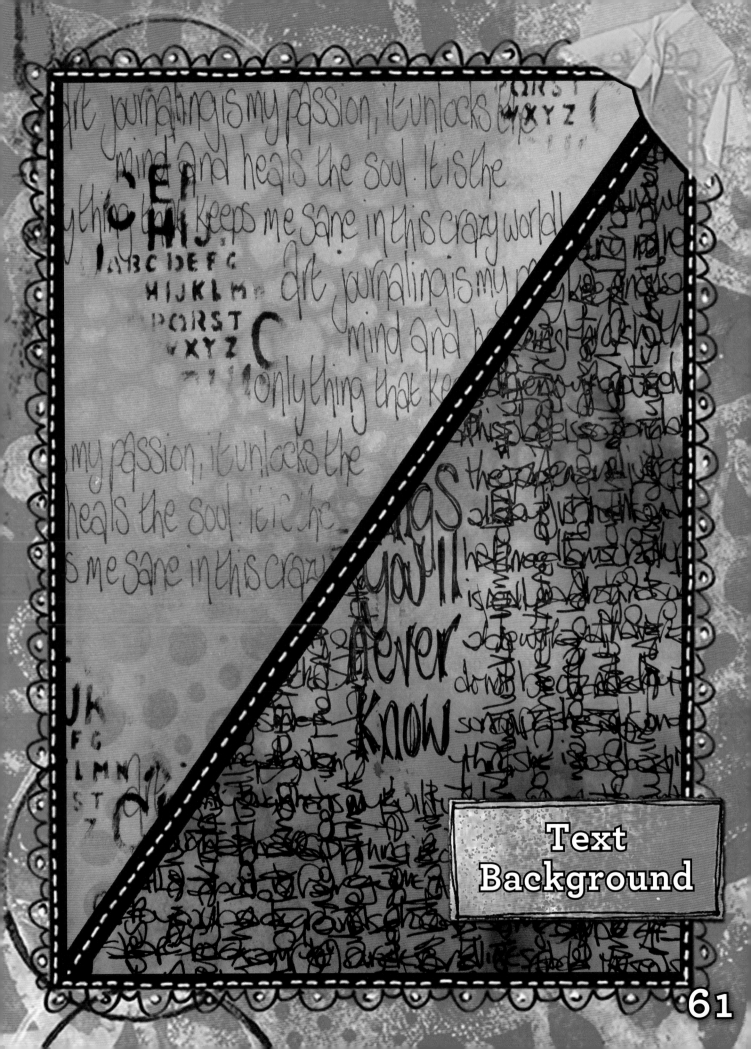

Text
Background

61

1. Ink a text stamp with Jet Black Archival Ink.

2. Stamp randomly over the inked page.

1. Write a few words in the middle of an inked page.

2. Write continuously from left to right across the page.

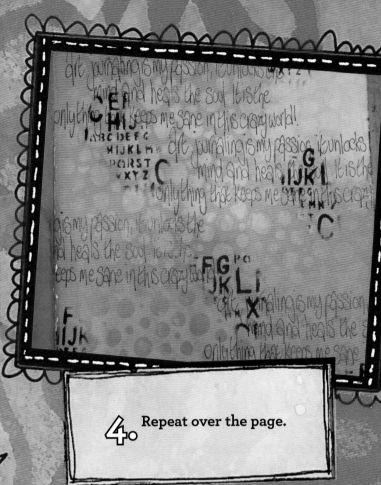

3. Take an alphabet stencil and stencil through with Black Marble Dylusions Paint and a Ranger Mini Ink Blending tool.

4. Repeat over the page.

3. Keep going until you reach the bottom of the page.

4. Turn the page 90 degrees and continue writing.

Graphic Shapes

A simple way to add more interest to your backgrounds without over facing them is to add some simple graphic shapes, for example circles and lines. I add these using black and white ink. Black and white are not technically colours so they always make your work pop. When adding circles I prefer to use odd numbers, 1, 3 and 5 as I feel it is more aesthetically pleasing. The number will depend on how big the circle is you are applying. If the circles are big, not many are needed. So what do I make these circles with? Is there a special tool to use? Err, no. I use whatever is in front of me...the lid of a dabber paint, gesso jar, the bottom of my take out drink container or the bottom of my soda can. At home, I have collected lids, etc. of various sizes ready to use but when I am on my travels everything is fair game. For adding lines, I use the straight edge of a Craft Scraper. Dip it onto the pad into the ink and holding it at 90 degrees to the page slowly pull towards you leaving a straight line of ink. The slower you move the Craft Scraper, the better effect you will get. Vary the length and quantity of your lines from page to page. In my studio I have one of my Spray Ink Pads filled totally with Black Marble ink and one filled totally with White Linen. I find these extremely useful and easy to use, but when traveling or teaching I spritz a little amount onto my Craft Sheet and dip my circles into it.

Another premise that I always stick to with, adding graphic shapes, is to have them following horizontal and vertical lines. To me, diagonal lines in a background imply movement and lead the eye out and off the page. Therefore, everything I do goes horizontally or vertically. It is by no means straight. Your lines can be tipsy, but not drunk. If you tried to put everything perfectly straight you are setting yourself up for a fall. A little bit of a wave, looks good and is so much more attainable.

Supplies Used:

Dylusions Black Marble Ink Spray
Dylusions White Linen Ink Spray
Ranger Craft Scraper
Various Sizes of Lids

Graphic
Shapes

1. Spritz a little Black Marble Ink Spray onto the Craft Sheet.

2. Dip something circular into the black ink and make a circle onto the inked journal page.

5. Holding the Craft Scraper at right angles make some horizontal and vertical lines.

6. Clean the mat and spritz White Linen Ink Spray onto the Craft Sheet.

3. Add more circles using an odd number.

4. Take a Craft Scraper and dip into the remaining ink.

7. Moving slightly to one side, make more circles like a highlight.

8. Add white lines to one side of the black.

Collage

Collage is one of my favourite ways to add imagery to a journal page and one that I have been doing since childhood. I spent many hours cutting, collecting and sticking for no apparent reason apart from the fact I enjoyed it. Finally I have found a home for it all, in my art journals.

A collage is a collection of ephemera glued down onto a surface, journal page or canvas. Collage materials can be magazines, tickets, ephemera, old photos, wrapping paper, old documents, doilies, stamps, letters, old book pages, maps, dress patterns, all kinds of paper that takes your fancy. I don't use newspaper as the ink bleeds but you can always use photocopies of almost anything. Collage can be used to create a whole background or to enhance an inked background. For example, as a border or as the main image and focal point. I mainly concentrate on borders and images, preferring my inked backgrounds to show through. For borders, I look through magazines for anything of interest that may be colourful or textured and cut it into small squares or oblongs, e.g. fabric design from a dress, curly hair from a model, grass from a garden photo. Sometimes I will limit myself to one colour and find as many textures in that colour as I can.

A typical way of mine for making borders is with collage sheets. These are ready-made sheets you can buy to cut up and use. They are made using scans of journal pages, already made into shapes for you. After making a border, I like to outline it all with a doodle to make it bed down into the page, before adding a quote or a main image.

Supplies Used:

Imagery
Ranger Collage Glue Stick
Black Pen

WHEN
THE
BRIGHT,
STARS
SHINE

Collage

1. Cut out lots of square and oblong shapes, from images in magazines etc.

2. Position them around the edge of an inked journal page.

5. Look through the magazine for an image that can be used as a body but isn't a body.

6. Stick the images down and add extras like arms, glasses, eyes or a hat.

3. When happy, stick them all down with a glue stick.

4. Cut out a head and a pair of legs from a magazine.

7. Find some random wording and cut into strips.

8. Outline everything with a black pen to incorporate it to the page and add doodling.

Doodling

How do you even start to explain doodling? To me it is something that comes instinctively every time I hold a pen or a pencil in my hand. I have the sudden urge to make marks on paper or in my journal. I call it taking my pen for a walk! My best doodling is done when my mind is on other things. It helps me concentrate. I was the annoying child who always appeared to be distracted in class, when in reality the only way to make my mind still and able to concentrate was to doodle, much to the chagrin of my teachers. I listen to audible books whilst doodling, and the combination of the two really calms me. Apparently doing both at the same time means I am using every part of my brain, therefore it is in balance. An equally balanced brain means that I cannot have a manic attack, of which I am prone...happy days. If you ever see me on an aeroplane, beach, waiting room or by the pool, you will no doubt find me doodling and listening to forensic crime with a big calm satisfied look on my face. I will be in my zone. So what to doodle? A straight line is a doodle. A circle is a doodle. A zig zag is a doodle. Start with two straight lines and doodle the same simple pattern in between them. Draw another two lines and this time, doodle another simple design then repeat with the first doodle again. I like to keep all my doodling simple, I think it is far better to doodle a few simple designs well than fill the page with lots of complicated designs not particularly well executed. Start small and you will soon get the hang of it and before long you will be like me doodling inside the doodles, lol.

My favourite type of doodling is always with a white pen onto black surface. It makes the doodling really pop. Otherwise it is nearly always with a black pen onto almost finished journal pages. I doodle on the background, in the foreground, on the main image, round the border, in fact everywhere often repeating it all again with a white pen.
I doodle until I am all doodled out!

Supplies Used:

Selection of Black & White Pens
Black Marble Dylusions Paint
Ranger Mini Ink Blending Tool
Dylusions Journal Block
Dylusions Silhouette Mask

Doodling

doodle love.

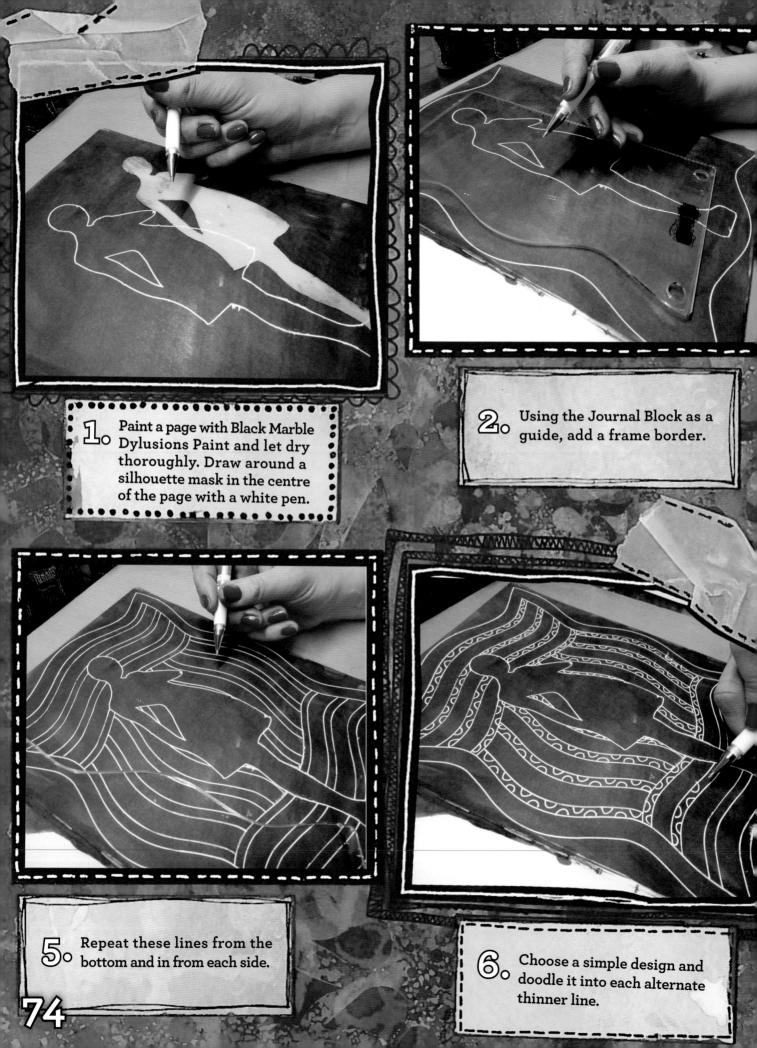

1. Paint a page with Black Marble Dylusions Paint and let dry thoroughly. Draw around a silhouette mask in the centre of the page with a white pen.

2. Using the Journal Block as a guide, add a frame border.

5. Repeat these lines from the bottom and in from each side.

6. Choose a simple design and doodle it into each alternate thinner line.

3. Repeat about 1/2" in to make a thick frame.

4. Starting at the top of the page, add thick and thin lines with the Journal Block.

7. Choose a different simple design for the remaining thicker lines.

8. Doodle around the outside of the frame and add faux stitch lines inside.

Journaling Basics:
The What's & How's

These are the two main questions I get asked over and over again. Nobody knows where to start and almost everyone tells me that it terrifies them. So let me begin by telling you that you don't have to write anything if you don't want to. The word "journal" does not mean "to write"; it actually means "to record". To keep a record of things. There is nothing profound about journaling, nothing deep, you don't have to have a degree in English Literature or an A+ in philosophy. You just need to want to write. Pure and simple!! If you want to write about it then write, if you don't then don't.

My journals are art journals, full of my art and most of the time they have some writing on them. But for a long time they didn't. They just contained art!! But over time I realised that words added to the art and in fact became part of the art itself. When I was working out a lot of things that were stuck in my head, I felt an intense need to write and I would fill the pages with my rantings and ramblings. Once I started, the floodgates opened and I couldn't stop. Page after page, after page. But then I would panic in case anyone could read what I had put. As a consequence I became very adept at hiding parts of my writing. With images, paint, stamps and doodling. I wrote smaller, then bigger, then loopier, then round in a spiral, then upside down! It became my mission to come up with as many different ways as I could! Then I realised that no one was actually reading it anyway! (insert wry smile). We all worry what people think of us when in fact they rarely do!

If you are stuck on what to write, then just start with simple things, like a quote, the lyrics to your favourite song, a psalm or prayer. All things that you don't have to really think about. Then progress to how your day was, where you would like to go on holiday, your dream house. When you realise that writing is a lot easier than you thought, then you can start writing about things that bother/trouble you. Get it out onto the paper, you can always paint over it, stick images on top or even stick two pages together! I don't write for the purpose of reading it again. I journal for the purpose of emptying my head, it makes me feel lighter. A concern I hear all the time is.."I don't like my handwriting..." Two things you can do to alter that...make your writing better or disguise it. People keep telling me how nice my writing is, but I have spent years practising the shapes and letters. It was part of my OCD. I would carefully draw each shape again and again until I got it right. It doesn't just happen, practise is the key.

If you just want to disguise your writing, I find the loopier and faster you write the better. I pay no attention to spelling, grammar or punctuation, and I rarely leave gaps between, preferring to just let the words flow. Your handwriting is part of what makes you "you" and therefore should be a big part of your journal.

Journaling Basics:
Supplies

The main supplies that I use in my journaling are pens, journal line stamps and my Journal Block.

Pens: I use a wide variety of pens in all sizes, mainly black and white. I like to use waterproof pens as I am never sure if I am going to add anything else over the top of the writing. I also mainly use water-based pens, as I am very sensitive to the smell of oil and solvent based ones. I have tons of each pen with me at all times, so that I don't run out! When I am flying I have a brush roll that is filled with just black and white pens (40 all together, and most of them have to be new). That sounds like a lot, I know, but sometimes my journey can take up to 15 to 20 hours and I would cry if I ran out!

These are my favourites, in no particular order.

Black: *Posca Paint Markers 1mr and 3m*: For filling in all of my designs. *Uni Pin 0.4/0.5/0.8 Fine Liners*: These are great for sketching out my doodled letters. *Pilot Varsity Pen*: Has a faux cartridge pen nib and is fabulous for writing with. *Fude Ball 1.5*: This pen is the only pen I know that just glides over painted areas. *Black Glaze Sakura*: This pen leaves a slightly raised image. Fabulous for outlining things and making them look embossed. *Sharpie Markers: Fine line and bullet*: Great on magazine images and also the covers of my journals.

White: *Posca Paint Markers*: Mainly for filling in and outlining letters. *Signo Uniball*: I use this for most of my white pen work, but it can sometimes take a while to dry. *Sakura Gelly Roll*: This dries really quick but not as creamy as the *Signo Sakura Souffle*: Leaves a nice raised but matte outline.

Journal Line Stamps: These are stamps that I drew especially for people to journal in between. Writing onto a blank page can be scary but if you have a clear guide of where to put your writing it can dispel the fear. Even though I can draw in my own journal lines, I find it is far quicker to use my stamps! I always stamp with Ranger Jet Black Archival Ink, so I can colour in with my inks later if I wish.

Journal Block: The Dylusions Journal block has a straight edge and a wavy edge and both can be used for creating journal lines. You just position the block on the page and draw along the edge onto the page. Keeping the block in the same position on a page but moving the wavy edge down a bit will result in parallel wavy lines. Alternately flipping the wavy edge around will.

Journaling

One of the easiest ways to start your journaling/writing is by having guides on the page to write in between. I have a lot of stamps specially made for this purpose; some are straight, some are wavy. Sometimes I stamp a few of the same and sometimes I combine a few of them together. This gives you somewhere definite to start. Normally, I will start journaling at the top of the page, filling in alternate lines with writing. If I get to the bottom and have more to write then I go back and fill in the other lines. If I don't want people to easily read what I have written I will turn the page around to write, then it will appear upside down.

Soon you will have the confidence to write without journaling guidelines. Try varying the width of your lines for a different effect. When you can't think of anything to write, just start with what's in your head, what's your day been like, anything!! The important thing is not the subject but the actual writing. Just the very act of writing will usually kick start imagination. Don't feel that your writing needs to relate to images on your page. My journaling is often added months after the page was created. Start a quote book. I always have a notebook on me, in which I jot down any quotes that catch my eye. When I'm stuck for words I just pull out one of the books, and flick through the pages 'til I find a suitable one. And remember, there are no rules.

If you don't feel like writing - then don't. The art journal police are far too busy with other things than to come to check your art. It's your journal, you're free to do anything you like!

Supplies Used:

Dylusions Creative Journal
Ranger Jet Black Archival Ink
Line Stamp
Black Pen

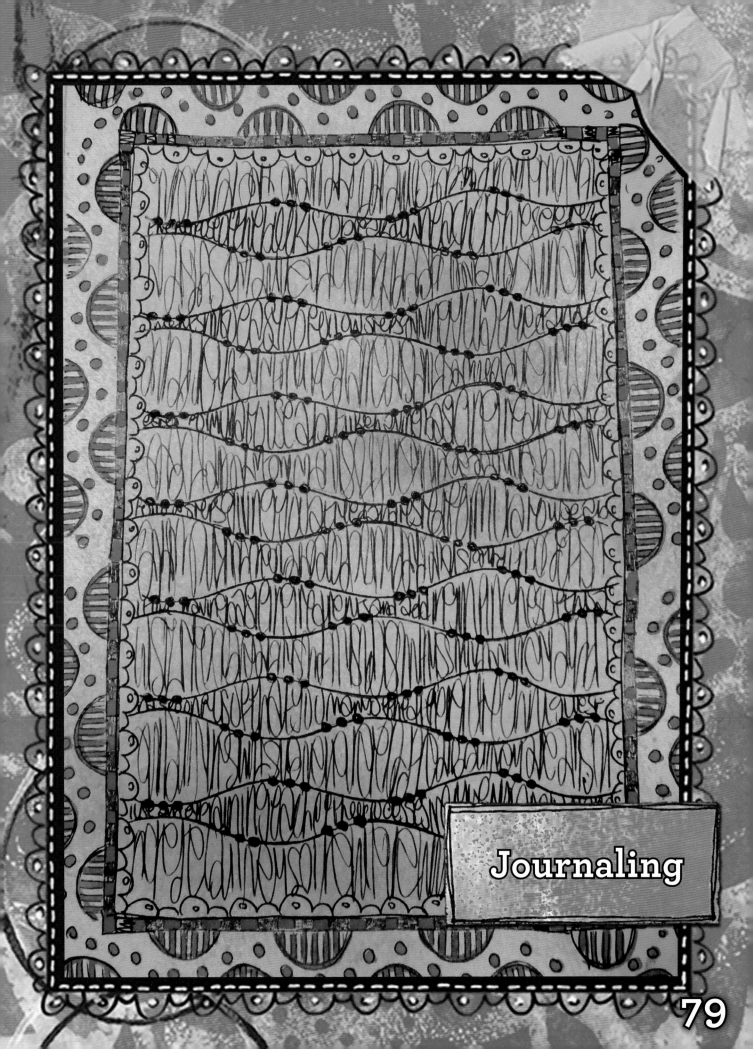

Journaling

1. Ink the journal line stamp with black ink and stamp onto the page.

2. Repeat across the page.

3. Start writing, leaving no gaps between words and no punctuation. Try to have each letter touch the top and bottom of the journal lines.

4. Write in every other journal line. Turn the page upside down and continue writing.

Notes to Self

Notes to Self

83